EASY
Tapas

EASY
Tapas

Love Food ® is an imprint of Parragon Books Ltd

Parragon
Queen Street House
4 Queen Street
Bath BA1 1HE, UK

Copyright © Parragon Books Ltd 2009

Love Food ® and the accompanying heart device is a trademark of Parragon Books Ltd

Introduction by Susanna Tee
Additional photography by Clive Streeter
Additional food styling by Angela Drake

ISBN: 978-1-4075-5632-1

Printed in Indonesia

NOTES FOR THE READER
• This book uses imperial, metric, and US cup measurements. Follow the same units of measurement throughout; do not mix imperial and metric.
• All spoon measurements are level: teaspoons are assumed to be 5 ml, and tablespoons are assumed to be 15 ml.
• Unless otherwise stated, milk is assumed to be low-fat and eggs are medium. The times given are an approximate guide only.
• Some recipes contain nuts. If you are allergic to nuts, you should avoid using them and any products containing nuts.
• Recipes using raw or very lightly cooked eggs should be avoided by infants, the elderly, pregnant women, convalescents, and anyone with a chronic illness.

Contents

Introduction

Tapas, those little tempting morsels of food, are found on almost every bar counter in Spain. Eating them, accompanied with a glass of dry sherry, chilled white wine, or a beer, before lunch or dinner, is a part of everyday Spanish life. It is an informal way of eating and, in Spain, the tapas experience accompanies friendship and conversation. There is even the Spanish tradition of *el tapeo,* or "eating tapas," when friends stroll from one bar to another, customarily standing, talking, drinking, and sampling the house specialties of each.

The History of Tapas

The Spanish word *tapas* means "lid" or "cover" and it is from Andalusia that the most commonly cited explanation originates. It is thought that Andalusian innkeepers put a slice of bread on top of glasses of sherry or wine to keep out the fruit flies and dust between sips. This led to the addition of a slice of ham or cheese to make it a snack and then to more elaborate toppings to attract customers, and hence tapas were created.

The Culinary Repertoire

The variety of ingredients and dishes, both hot and cold, that make up tapas are enormous. There are, of course, delicious combinations piled on bread or toast. In addition, there are fried vegetables and fish, meatballs, croquettes, fritters, omelets, tapas on toothpicks, and ingredients cooked in a sauce. It is also rare not to include one or two types of olives as well as crusty bread to eat with sauce-based tapas. Bowls of salted almonds, chunks of Manchego cheese, and chorizo sausage are always popular. Vegetables, particularly tomatoes, eggplant, bell peppers, and potatoes, fresh meat and poultry, cured meats, dairy produce, and usually one or more fish or shellfish are all part of this culinary experience.

Serving Tapas

Tapas have now evolved into an entire cuisine, and in cafés, restaurants, and the home, a selection of these delicious miniature morsels can be a meal in themselves. For an informal lunch or supper party, serve about six different types of tapas dishes, choosing your selection from the different chapters in this book. Select a variety of hot and cold tapas and include a selection of simple tapas, such as bowls of olives, almonds, cheese, and chorizo sausage. These simple tapas are also ideal to serve with predinner drinks.

Tapas dishes are the perfect, easy dish to serve as an appetizer at a dinner party or as a light lunch dish. In these instances, halve the number of servings that the recipe suggests it serves and accompany with Spanish bread and a salad. In addition, tapas are ideal for serving at an informal party. Allow eight to ten servings per person and multiply quantities of the recipes, as necessary. For these occasions, you will find that not only are the recipes easy to prepare but they can also be prepared in advance.

Essential Ingredients

Almonds A bowl of blanched almonds is one of the easiest tapas to make. For freshness, buy unblanched almonds and blanch just before using—just drop the nuts into boiling water for a few minutes, then drain and refresh under cold water. Use your fingers to squeeze the nuts so they pop out of their skins.

Cheese For a typical tapas ingredient, keep the traditional Manchego cheese, a sheep's milk cheese from La Mancha, and cubes of Cabrales, a rich bleu cheese, to serve with drinks.

Cured Meats Serrano or mountain ham, perhaps the best known, features at many tapas bars—it can be served in thin slices, as a sandwich filling or on bread topped with vegetables. The most highly regarded cured hams are labeled as Iberico and can be identified by the hefty price! Other popular cured meats are pork loin and Spain's ubiquitous pork sausage—the spicy chorizo.

Garlic An essential Spanish flavoring. Buy fresh and use within a month once the head has been broken into.

Olive Oil Olive oil is a regular feature of Spanish cooking. Heat destroys the flavor of oil so save your best extra virgin oil for uncooked dishes and cook with plain olive oil.

Paprika Made from ground, dried red bell peppers, paprika adds a mild or strong smoky flavor and vibrant red color to dishes.

Legumes Spanish kitchen cupboards contain many jars and cans of legumes, cooked and ready to use without first having to go to the trouble of overnight soaking and boiling.

Canned Fish There is a wide selection of canned fish available, including anchovies, sardines, and tuna. Buy fish preserved in oil for the best flavor.

1

Little Bites

Cracked Marinated Olives

serves 8

1 lb/450 g can or jar
unpitted large green
Spanish olives, drained

4 garlic cloves, peeled

2 tsp coriander seeds

1 small lemon

4 sprigs of fresh thyme

4 feathery stalks of fennel

2 small fresh red chiles
(optional)

extra virgin olive oil

pepper

To allow the flavors of the marinade to penetrate the olives, place on a cutting board and, using a rolling pin, bash them lightly so that they crack slightly. Alternatively, use a sharp knife to cut a lengthwise slit in each olive as far as the pit. Using the flat side of a broad knife, lightly crush each garlic clove. Using a mortar and pestle, crack the coriander seeds. Cut the lemon, with its rind, into small chunks.

Put the olives, garlic, coriander seeds, lemon chunks, thyme sprigs, fennel, and chiles, if using, in a large bowl and toss together. Season with pepper to taste, but you should not need to add salt as preserved olives are usually salty enough. Pack the ingredients tightly into a glass jar with a lid. Pour in enough olive oil to cover the olives, then seal the jar tightly.

Let the olives stand at room temperature for 24 hours, then marinate in the refrigerator for at least 1 week but preferably 2 weeks before serving. From time to time, gently give the jar a shake to remix the ingredients. Return the olives to room temperature and remove from the oil to serve. Provide wooden toothpicks for spearing the olives.

Olives with Orange & Lemon

serves 4–6

2 tsp fennel seeds

2 tsp cumin seeds

1¼ cups green Spanish olives

1¼ cups black Spanish olives

2 tsp grated orange rind

2 tsp grated lemon rind

3 shallots, finely chopped

pinch of ground cinnamon

4 tbsp white wine vinegar

5 tbsp Spanish extra virgin olive oil

2 tbsp orange juice

1 tbsp chopped fresh mint

1 tbsp chopped fresh parsley

Dry-roast the fennel seeds and cumin seeds in a small, heavy-bottom skillet, shaking the skillet frequently, until they begin to pop and give off their aroma. Remove the skillet from the heat and let cool.

Place the olives, orange and lemon rinds, shallots, cinnamon, and roasted seeds in a bowl.

Whisk the vinegar, olive oil, orange juice, mint, and parsley together in a bowl and pour over the olives. Toss well, then cover and let chill for 1–2 days before serving.

Salted Almonds

serves 6

4 tbsp Spanish olive oil

8 oz/225 g whole almonds, blanched

coarse sea salt

1 tsp paprika or ground cumin (optional)

Preheat the oven to 350°F/180°C. Place the olive oil in a roasting pan and swirl it around so that it covers the bottom. Add the almonds and toss them in the pan so that they are evenly coated in the oil, then spread them out in a single layer.

Roast the almonds in the preheated oven for 20 minutes, or until they are light golden brown, tossing several times during the cooking. Drain the almonds on paper towels, then transfer them to a bowl.

While the almonds are still warm, sprinkle with plenty of sea salt and paprika, if using, and toss together to coat. Serve the almonds warm or cold. The almonds are at their best when served freshly cooked so, if possible, cook them on the day that you plan to eat them. However, they can be stored in an airtight container for up to 3 days.

Sautéed Garlic Mushrooms

serves 6

1 lb/450 g white mushrooms

5 tbsp olive oil

2 garlic cloves, finely chopped

squeeze of lemon juice

4 tbsp chopped fresh flat-leaf parsley, chopped, plus extra sprigs to garnish

salt and pepper

Wipe or brush clean the mushrooms, then trim off the stalks close to the caps. Cut any large mushrooms in half or into quarters. Heat the olive oil in a large, heavy-bottom skillet, add the garlic, and cook for 30 seconds–1 minute, or until lightly browned. Add the mushrooms and sauté over high heat, stirring most of the time, until the mushrooms have absorbed all the oil in the skillet.

Reduce the heat to low. When the juices have come out of the mushrooms, increase the heat again, and sauté for 4–5 minutes, stirring most of the time, until the juices have almost evaporated. Add a squeeze of lemon juice and season to taste with salt and pepper. Stir in the parsley and cook for an additional minute.

Transfer the sautéed mushrooms to a warmed serving dish and serve piping hot or warm, garnished with parsley sprigs.

Patatas Bravas

serves 6

2 lb 4 oz/1 kg potatoes

Spanish olive oil,
for pan-frying

salt

for the sauce

1 onion, finely chopped

2 garlic cloves, crushed

¼ cup white wine or dry
Spanish sherry

14 oz/400 g canned
chopped tomatoes

2 tsp white or red wine
vinegar

1–2 tsp crushed dried
chiles

2 tsp hot or sweet smoked
Spanish paprika

To make the sauce, heat 2 tablespoons of oil in a pan, then add the onion and cook over medium heat, stirring occasionally, for 5 minutes, or until softened but not browned. Add the garlic and cook, stirring, for 30 seconds. Add the wine and bring to a boil. Add the tomatoes, vinegar, chiles, and paprika, then reduce the heat and simmer, uncovered, for 10–15 minutes, or until a thick sauce forms.

When the sauce is cooked, use a handheld blender to blend until smooth. Alternatively, transfer the sauce to a food processor and process until smooth. Return the sauce to the pan and set aside.

Do not peel the potatoes, but cut them into chunky pieces. Heat enough oil in a large skillet to come about 1 inch/2.5 cm up the side of the skillet. Add the potato pieces and cook over medium–high heat, turning occasionally, for 10–15 minutes until golden brown. Remove with a slotted spoon and drain on paper towels, then sprinkle with salt.

Meanwhile, gently reheat the sauce. Transfer the potatoes to a warmed serving dish and drizzle over the sauce. Serve hot, with wooden toothpicks to spear the potatoes.

Baby Potatoes with Aïoli

serves 6–8

1 lb/450 g baby new potatoes

prepared aïoli, to coat

1 tbsp chopped fresh parsley

salt

To prepare the potatoes, cut them in half or quarters to make bite-size pieces. If they are very small, you can leave them whole. Put the potatoes in a large pan of cold, salted water and bring to a boil. Lower the heat and let simmer for 7 minutes, or until just tender. Drain well, then turn out into a large bowl.

While the potatoes are still warm, pour over the aïoli sauce to coat and gently toss the potatoes in it. Adding the sauce to the potatoes while they are still warm will help them to absorb the garlic flavor. Let stand for about 20 minutes to allow the potatoes to marinate in the sauce.

Transfer the potatoes with aïoli to a warmed serving dish, sprinkle over the parsley and salt to taste, and serve warm. Alternatively, the aïoli can be served separately, allowing diners to dip the potatoes themselves.

Potato & Spinach Triangles

serves 4

2 tbsp butter, melted, plus extra for greasing

8 oz/225 g waxy potatoes, finely diced

1 lb 2 oz/500 g fresh baby spinach

2 tbsp water

1 tomato, seeded and chopped

¼ tsp chili powder

½ tsp lemon juice

8 oz/225 g (8 sheets) filo pastry, thawed if frozen

salt and pepper

Preheat the oven to 375°F/190°C. Lightly grease a baking sheet with a little butter. Cook the potatoes in a pan of lightly salted boiling water for 10 minutes, or until tender. Drain thoroughly and place in a mixing bowl.

Meanwhile, put the spinach into a large skillet with the water, cover, and cook, stirring occasionally, over low heat for 2 minutes, or until wilted. Drain the spinach thoroughly, squeezing out the excess moisture, and add to the potatoes. Stir in the tomato, chili powder, and lemon juice. Season to taste with salt and pepper.

Lightly brush the sheets of filo pastry with melted butter. Spread out 4 of the sheets and lay a second sheet on top of each. Cut them into rectangles about 8 x 4 inches/ 20 x 10 cm.

Spoon a portion of the potato-and-spinach mixture onto one end of each rectangle. Fold a corner of the pastry over the filling, fold the pointed end back over the pastry strip, then fold over the remaining pastry to form a triangle.

Place the triangles on the prepared baking sheet and bake in the preheated oven for 20 minutes, or until golden brown. Serve hot or cold.

Tapenade

serves 4

3½ oz/100 g canned anchovy fillets

12 oz/350 g black olives, pitted and coarsely chopped

2 garlic cloves, coarsely chopped

2 tbsp capers, drained and rinsed

1 tbsp Dijon mustard

3 tbsp extra virgin olive oil

2 tbsp lemon juice

slices toasted country bread, to serve

Drain the anchovies, reserving the oil from the can. Coarsely chop the fish and place in the blender. Add the reserved oil and all the remaining ingredients. Process to a smooth paste. Stop and scrape down the sides if necessary.

Transfer the tapenade to a dish, cover with plastic wrap, and chill in the refrigerator until required. If you are not planning to use the tapenade until the following day (or even the one after), cover the surface with a layer of olive oil to prevent it from drying out. Serve with slices of toasted country bread.

Fresh Mint & Bean Pâté

serves 12

1 lb 12 oz/800 g fresh fava beans in their pods, shelled to give about 12 oz/350 g

8 oz/225 g soft goat cheese

1 garlic clove, crushed

2 scallions, finely chopped

1 tbsp Spanish extra virgin olive oil, plus extra to serve

grated rind and 2 tbsp lemon juice

about 60 large fresh mint leaves, about ½ oz/15 g in total

12 slices of baguette

salt and pepper

Cook the fava beans in a pan of boiling water for 8–10 minutes, or until tender. Drain well and let cool. When the beans are cool enough to handle, slip off their skins and put the beans in a food processor. This is a laborious task, but worth doing if you have the time. This quantity will take about 15 minutes to skin.

Add the goat cheese, garlic, scallions, oil, lemon rind and juice, and mint leaves to the fava beans and process until well mixed. Season the pâté to taste with salt and pepper. Turn into a bowl, cover, then chill in the refrigerator for at least 1 hour before serving.

To serve, preheat the broiler to high. Toast the baguette slices under the broiler until golden brown on both sides. Drizzle a little oil over the toasted bread slices, then spread the pâté on top and serve immediately.

Simmered Summer Vegetables

serves 6–8

1 large eggplant

4 tbsp Spanish olive oil

1 onion, thinly sliced

2 garlic cloves, finely chopped

2 zucchini, thinly sliced

1 red bell pepper, cored, seeded, and thinly sliced

1 green bell pepper, cored, seeded, and thinly sliced

8 tomatoes, peeled, seeded, and chopped

salt and pepper

chopped fresh flat-leaf parsley, to garnish

slices thick country bread, to serve (optional)

Cut the eggplant into 1-inch/2.5-cm cubes. Heat the oil in a large ovenproof casserole, then add the onion and cook over medium heat, stirring occasionally, for 5 minutes, or until softened but not browned. Add the garlic and cook, stirring, for 30 seconds, or until softened.

Increase the heat to medium–high, then add the eggplant cubes and cook, stirring occasionally, for 10 minutes, or until softened and beginning to brown. Add the zucchini and bell peppers and cook, stirring occasionally, for 10 minutes, or until softened. Add the tomatoes and season to taste with salt and pepper.

Bring the mixture to a boil, then reduce the heat, cover, and simmer, stirring occasionally so that the vegetables do not stick to the bottom of the pan, for 15–20 minutes, or until tender. If necessary, uncover, then increase the heat and cook to evaporate any excess liquid, as the mixture should be thick.

Serve hot or cold, garnished with chopped parsley and accompanied by bread slices, if using, for scooping up the vegetables.

Fava Bean Salad

serves 4

5 lb 8 oz/2.5 kg young fava beans or 15 oz/425 g frozen fava beans

2 tomatoes, peeled, seeded, and diced

3 tbsp shredded basil

1¾ oz/50 g Parmesan shavings

for the dressing

1 tsp white wine vinegar

1 small garlic clove, crushed

4 tbsp extra virgin olive oil

salt and pepper

Bring a large pan of water to a boil. Add the beans, bring back to a boil, then cook for 3 minutes, until just tender. Drain and tip into a serving dish or arrange on individual plates.

Whisk the dressing ingredients and spoon over the beans while still warm.

Scatter over the diced tomato, basil, and Parmesan shavings. Serve immediately, at room temperature, in a warmed bowl.

Spicy Tomato Salad

serves 4

4 large ripe tomatoes

1 small fresh red chile

1 garlic clove

2/3 cup fresh basil

4 tbsp extra virgin olive oil

1 tbsp lemon juice

2 tbsp balsamic vinegar

salt and pepper

fresh basil sprigs,
to garnish

fresh crusty bread,
to serve

Bring a kettle or saucepan of water to a boil. Place the tomatoes in a heatproof bowl, then pour over enough boiling water to cover them. Let them soak for 2–4 minutes, then lift out of the water and cool slightly.

When the tomatoes are cool enough to handle, gently pierce the skins with the tip of a knife. The skins should now be easy to remove. Discard the skins, then chop the tomatoes and place them in a large salad bowl.

Seed and finely chop the chile, then chop the garlic. Rinse and finely chop the basil, then add it to the tomatoes in the bowl with the chile and the garlic.

Mix the oil, lemon juice, and balsamic vinegar together in a separate bowl, then season to taste with salt and pepper. Pour the mixture over the salad and toss together well. Garnish with basil sprigs and serve immediately with fresh crusty bread.

Stuffed Cherry Tomatoes

serves 8

24 cherry tomatoes

for the anchovy & olive filling

1¾ oz/50 g canned anchovy fillets in olive oil

8 pimiento-stuffed green Spanish olives, finely chopped

2 large hard-cooked eggs, finely chopped

pepper

for the crab filling

6 oz/175 g canned crabmeat, drained

4 tbsp mayonnaise

1 tbsp chopped fresh flat-leaf parsley

salt and pepper

paprika, for garnish

for the olive & caper filling

12 pitted black Spanish olives

3 tbsp capers

6 tbsp aïoli

salt and pepper

If necessary, cut and discard a very thin slice from the stem end of each tomato to make the bases flat and stable. Cut a thin slice from the smooth end of each cherry tomato and discard. Using a serrated knife or teaspoon, loosen the pulp and seeds of each and scoop out, discarding the flesh. Turn the scooped-out tomatoes upside down on paper towels and let drain for 5 minutes.

To make the anchovy and olive filling, drain the anchovies, reserving the olive oil for later, then chop finely and place in a bowl. Add the olives and hard-cooked eggs. Pour in a trickle of the reserved olive oil to moisten the mixture, then season with pepper. (Don't add salt to season, as the anchovies are salty.) Mix well together.

To make the crab mayonnaise filling, place the crabmeat, mayonnaise, and parsley in a bowl and mix well together. Season the filling to taste with salt and pepper. Sprinkle with paprika before serving.

To make the olive and caper filling, place the olives and capers on paper towels to drain them well, then chop finely and place in a bowl. Add the aïoli and mix well together. Season the filling to taste with salt and pepper.

Fill a pastry bag fitted with a ¾-inch/2-cm plain tip with the filling of your choice and use to fill the hollow tomato shells. Store the cherry tomatoes in the refrigerator until ready to serve.

Pickled Stuffed Bell Peppers

serves 6

7 oz/200 g Cuajada cheese, Queso del Tietar, or other fresh goat cheese

14 oz/400 g pickled sweet bell peppers or pimientos del piquillo, drained

1 tbsp finely chopped fresh dill

salt and pepper

Cut the cheese into pieces about ½ inch/1 cm long. Slit the sides of the sweet bell peppers and seed, if you like. Stuff the bell peppers with the cheese.

Arrange the stuffed bell peppers on serving plates. Sprinkle with the dill and season to taste with salt and pepper. Cover and chill until ready to serve.

Roasted Bell Peppers & Tomatoes

serves 4

2 red bell peppers

2 yellow bell peppers

2 orange bell peppers

4 tomatoes, halved

1 tbsp olive oil

3 garlic cloves, chopped

1 onion, sliced in rings

2 tbsp fresh thyme

salt and pepper

Halve and seed the bell peppers. Place them, cut-side down, on a cookie sheet and cook under a preheated broiler for 10 minutes. Add the tomatoes to the cookie sheet and broil for 5 minutes, until the skins of the bell peppers and tomatoes are charred.

Put the bell peppers into a plastic bag for 10 minutes to sweat, which will make the skin easier to peel. Remove the tomato skins and chop the flesh. Peel the skins from the bell peppers and slice the flesh into strips.

Heat the oil in a large skillet and fry the garlic and onion, stirring occasionally, for 3–4 minutes, or until softened. Add the bell peppers and tomatoes to the skillet and cook for 5 minutes. Stir in the fresh thyme and season to taste with salt and pepper.

Transfer to serving bowls and serve warm or chilled.

Zucchini Fritters with a Dipping Sauce

serves 6–8

1 lb/450 g baby zucchini

3 tbsp all-purpose flour

1 tsp paprika

1 large egg

2 tbsp milk

corn oil, for pan-frying

coarse sea salt

for the pine nut sauce

⅔ cup pine nuts

1 garlic clove, peeled

3 tbsp Spanish extra virgin olive oil

1 tbsp lemon juice

3 tbsp water

1 tbsp chopped fresh flat-leaf parsley

salt and pepper

To make the pine nut sauce, place the pine nuts and garlic in a food processor and process to form a paste. With the motor still running, gradually add the olive oil, lemon juice, and water to form a smooth sauce. Stir in the parsley and season to taste with salt and pepper.

Transfer to a serving bowl and reserve until needed. To prepare the zucchini, cut them on the diagonal into thin slices about ¼ inch/5 mm thick. Place the flour and paprika in a plastic bag and mix together. Beat the egg and milk together in a large bowl.

Add the zucchini slices to the flour mixture and toss well together until coated. Shake off the excess flour. Heat the corn oil in a large, heavy-bottom skillet to a depth of about ½ inch/1 cm. Dip the zucchini slices, one at a time, into the egg mixture, then slip them into the hot oil. Cook the zucchini slices in batches in a single layer so that they do not overcrowd the skillet, for 2 minutes, or until they are crisp and golden brown.

Using a slotted spoon, remove the zucchini fritters from the skillet and drain on paper towels. Continue until all the zucchini slices have been fried.

Serve the zucchini fritters piping hot, lightly sprinkled with sea salt, and accompanied by the pine nut sauce for dipping.

Marinated Eggplants

serves 4

2 eggplants, halved lengthwise

4 tbsp Spanish olive oil

2 garlic cloves, finely chopped

2 tbsp chopped fresh parsley

1 tbsp chopped fresh thyme

2 tbsp lemon juice

salt and pepper

Make 2–3 slashes in the flesh of the eggplant halves and place, cut-side down, in an ovenproof dish. Season to taste with salt and pepper, then pour over the olive oil and sprinkle with the garlic, parsley, and thyme. Cover and let marinate at room temperature for 2–3 hours.

Preheat the oven to 350°F/180°C. Uncover the dish and roast the eggplants in the preheated oven for 45 minutes. Remove the dish from the oven and turn the eggplants over. Baste with the cooking juices and sprinkle with the lemon juice. Return to the oven and cook for an additional 15 minutes.

Transfer the eggplants to serving plates. Spoon over the cooking juices and serve hot or warm.

Eggplant Rolls

serves 4

2 eggplants, sliced thinly lengthwise

5 tbsp olive oil

1 garlic clove, crushed

4 tbsp pesto

1½ cups mozzarella, grated

basil leaves, torn into pieces

salt and pepper

fresh basil leaves, to garnish

Preheat the oven to 350°F/180°C. Sprinkle the eggplant slices liberally with salt and let stand for 10–15 minutes to extract the bitter juices. Turn the slices over and repeat. Rinse well with cold water and drain on paper towels.

Heat the olive oil in a large skillet and add the garlic. Fry the eggplant slices lightly on both sides, a few at a time. Drain them on paper towels.

Spread the pesto onto one side of the eggplant slices. Top with the grated mozzarella and sprinkle with the torn basil leaves. Season with a little salt and pepper. Roll up the slices and secure with wooden toothpicks.

Arrange the eggplant rolls in a greased ovenproof baking dish. Place in the preheated oven and bake for 8–10 minutes.

Transfer the eggplant rolls to a warmed serving plate. Scatter with the basil sprigs and serve at once.

Chiles Rellenos

serves 4–8

3 eggs, separated

⅜ cup all-purpose flour

11½ oz/325 g cheddar or
other semihard cheese

16 fresh jalapeño chiles

corn oil, for deep-frying

Whisk the egg whites in a dry, grease-free bowl until stiff. Beat the egg yolks in a separate bowl, then fold in the whites. Spread out the flour in a shallow dish. Cut 8 oz/225 g of the cheese into 16 sticks and grate the remainder.

Make a slit in the side of each chile and scrape out the seeds. Rinse the cavities and pat dry with paper towels. Place a stick of cheese inside each chile.

Preheat the broiler. Heat the oil for deep-frying to 350–375°F/180–190°C, or until a cube of bread dropped into the oil browns in 30 seconds. Dip the chiles into the egg mixture, then into the flour. Deep-fry, turning occasionally, until golden brown all over. Drain well on paper towels.

Arrange the chiles in an ovenproof dish and sprinkle over the grated cheese. Place under the broiler until the cheese has melted, then serve.

Deep-Fried Artichoke Hearts

serves 4–6

½ cup self-rising flour

¼ tsp salt

¼ tsp hot or sweet smoked Spanish paprika

1 garlic clove, crushed

5 tbsp water

1 tbsp olive oil

juice of ½ lemon

12 small globe artichokes

sunflower or Spanish olive oil, for deep-frying

aïoli, to serve

To make the batter, put the flour, salt, paprika, and garlic in a large bowl and make a well in the center. Gradually pour the water and olive oil into the well and mix in the flour mixture from the side, beating constantly, until all the flour is incorporated and a smooth batter forms. Let rest while preparing the artichokes.

Fill a bowl with cold water and add the lemon juice. Cut off the stalks of the artichokes. With your hands, break off all the leaves, and carefully remove the choke (the mass of silky hairs) by pulling it out with your fingers or scooping it out with a spoon. Immediately put the artichoke hearts in the acidulated water to prevent discoloration.

Cook the artichoke hearts in a pan of boiling salted water for 15 minutes, or until tender but still firm, then drain well and pat dry with paper towels.

Heat enough sunflower or olive oil in a deep-fat fryer to 350–375°F/180–190°C, or until a cube of bread browns in 30 seconds. Spear an artichoke heart on a toothpick and dip into the batter, then drop the artichoke heart and toothpick into the hot oil. Cook the artichoke hearts, in batches to avoid overcrowding, for 1–2 minutes, or until golden brown and crisp. Remove with a slotted spoon or draining basket and drain on paper towels.

Serve hot, accompanied by a bowl of aïoli for dipping.

Meat
Dishes

Porterhouse Steak with Sherry

serves 6–8

4 porterhouse steaks, about
6–8 oz/175–225 g each
and 1 inch/2.5 cm thick

5 garlic cloves

3 tbsp Spanish olive oil

½ cup dry Spanish sherry

salt and pepper

chopped fresh flat-leaf
parsley, to garnish

Cut the steaks into 1-inch/2.5-cm cubes and put in a large, shallow dish. Slice 3 of the garlic cloves and set aside. Finely chop the remaining garlic cloves and sprinkle over the steak cubes. Season generously with pepper and mix together well. Cover and let marinate in the refrigerator for 1–2 hours.

Heat the oil in a large skillet, then add the garlic slices and cook over low heat, stirring, for 1 minute, or until golden brown. Increase the heat to medium–high, then add the steak cubes and cook, stirring constantly, for 2–3 minutes, or until browned and almost cooked to your liking.

Add the sherry and cook until it has evaporated slightly. Season to taste with salt and turn into a warmed serving dish. Garnish with chopped parsley and serve hot.

Beef Skewers with Orange Garlic

serves 6–8

3 tbsp white wine

2 tbsp Spanish olive oil

3 garlic cloves, finely chopped

juice of 1 orange

1 lb/450 g beef top round, cubed

1 lb/450 g pearl onions, halved

2 orange bell peppers, seeded and cut into squares

8 oz/225 g cherry tomatoes, halved

salt and pepper

Mix the wine, olive oil, garlic, and orange juice together in a shallow, nonmetallic dish. Add the cubes of beef, season to taste with salt and pepper, and toss to coat. Cover with plastic wrap and let marinate in the refrigerator for 2–8 hours.

Preheat the broiler to high. Drain the beef, reserving the marinade. Thread the beef, onions, bell peppers, and tomatoes alternately onto several small skewers.

Cook the skewers under the hot broiler, turning and brushing frequently with the marinade, for 10 minutes, or until cooked through. Transfer to warmed serving plates and serve immediately.

Spanish Meatballs with Cracked Olives

serves 6

2 oz/55 g day-old bread, crusts removed

3 tbsp water

1⅛ cups lean fresh ground pork

1⅛ cups lean fresh ground lamb

2 small onions, finely chopped

3 garlic cloves, crushed

1 tsp ground cumin

1 tsp ground coriander

1 egg, lightly beaten

all-purpose flour, for dusting

3 tbsp Spanish olive oil

14 oz/400 g canned chopped tomatoes

5 tbsp dry sherry or red wine

pinch of hot or sweet smoked Spanish paprika

pinch of sugar

1 cup cracked green Spanish olives in extra virgin olive oil

salt

crusty bread, to serve

Put the bread in a bowl, then add the water and let soak for 5 minutes. Using your hands, squeeze out as much of the water as possible from the bread and put the bread in a clean bowl. Add the ground meat, 1 chopped onion, 2 crushed garlic cloves, the cumin, coriander, and egg to the bread. Season to taste with salt and, using your hands, mix together well. Dust a plate or cookie sheet with flour. Using floured hands, roll the mixture into 30 equal-size, small balls, then put on the plate or cookie sheet and roll lightly in the flour.

Heat 2 tablespoons of the oil in a large skillet, then add the meatballs, in batches to avoid overcrowding, and cook over medium heat, turning frequently, for 8–10 minutes, until golden brown on all sides and firm. Remove with a slotted spoon and set aside.

Heat the remaining oil in the skillet, then add the remaining onion and cook, stirring occasionally, for 5 minutes, or until softened but not browned. Add the remaining garlic and cook, stirring, for 30 seconds. Add the tomatoes, sherry, paprika, and sugar and season to taste with salt. Bring to a boil, then reduce the heat and simmer for 10 minutes.

Using a handheld mixer, blend the tomato mixture until smooth. Return the sauce to the pan. Carefully return the meatballs to the skillet and add the olives. Simmer gently for 20 minutes, or until the meatballs are tender. Serve hot, with crusty bread to mop up the sauce.

Tiny Meatballs in Almond Sauce

serves 6–8

2 slices white bread, crusts
removed

3 tbsp water

1 lb/450 g freshly ground
pork

1 large onion, chopped

1 garlic clove, crushed

2 tbsp chopped fresh
flat-leaf parsley, plus
extra to garnish

1 egg, beaten

freshly grated nutmeg

all-purpose flour,
to coat

2 tbsp Spanish olive oil

lemon juice, to taste

salt and pepper

for the almond sauce

2 tbsp Spanish olive oil

1 slice white bread

scant 1 cup blanched
almonds

2 garlic cloves, finely
chopped

⅔ cup dry white wine

1¾ cups vegetable stock

To prepare the meatballs, place the bread in a bowl, then add the water and let soak for 5 minutes. With your hands, squeeze out the water and return the bread to a dry bowl. Add the ground pork, onion, garlic, parsley, and egg, then season with grated nutmeg and a little salt and pepper. Knead the ingredients well to form a smooth mixture.

Spread some flour on a plate. With floured hands, shape the meat mixture into about 30 equal-size balls, then roll each meatball in flour until coated. Heat the oil in a large, heavy-bottom skillet. Add the meatballs, in batches, and cook for 4–5 minutes. Using a slotted spoon, remove the meatballs from the skillet and reserve.

To make the sauce, heat the olive oil in the same skillet in which the meatballs were fried. Break the bread into pieces, add to the skillet with the almonds, and cook gently, stirring, until the bread and almonds are golden brown. Add the garlic and fry for an additional 30 seconds, then pour in the wine and boil for 1–2 minutes. Season to taste with salt and pepper and let cool slightly. Transfer to a food processor. Pour in the vegetable stock and process the mixture until smooth. Return the sauce to the skillet.

Carefully add the meatballs to the almond sauce and simmer for 25 minutes, or until the meatballs are tender. Taste the sauce and season with salt and pepper, if necessary. Transfer to a warmed serving dish, then add a squeeze of lemon juice to taste and sprinkle with chopped parsley. Serve immediately.

Calves' Liver in Almond Saffron Sauce

serves 6

4 tbsp Spanish olive oil

1 slice white bread

⅔ cup almonds, blanched

2 garlic cloves, crushed

pinch of saffron strands

⅔ cup dry Spanish sherry or white wine

1¼ cups vegetable stock

1 lb/450 g calves' liver

all-purpose flour, for dusting

salt and pepper

chopped fresh flat-leaf parsley, to garnish

crusty bread, to serve

To make the sauce, heat 2 tablespoons of the oil in a large skillet. Tear the bread into small pieces and add to the skillet with the almonds. Cook over low heat, stirring frequently, for 2 minutes, or until golden brown. Stir in the garlic and cook, stirring, for 30 seconds.

Add the saffron and sherry to the skillet and season to taste with salt and pepper.

Bring to a boil and continue to boil for 1–2 minutes. Remove from the heat and let cool slightly, then transfer the mixture to a food processor. Add the stock and process until smooth. Set aside.

Cut the liver into large bite-size pieces. Dust lightly with flour and season generously with pepper. Heat the remaining oil in the skillet, then add the liver and cook over medium heat, stirring constantly, for 2–3 minutes, or until firm and lightly browned.

Pour the sauce into the skillet and reheat gently for 1–2 minutes. Transfer to a warmed serving dish and garnish with chopped parsley. Serve hot, accompanied by chunks of crusty bread to mop up the sauce.

Lamb Skewers with Lemon

serves 8

2 garlic cloves, finely chopped

1 Spanish onion, finely chopped

2 tsp finely grated lemon rind

2 tbsp lemon juice

1 tsp fresh thyme leaves

1 tsp ground coriander

1 tsp ground cumin

2 tbsp red wine vinegar

½ cup Spanish olive oil

2 lb 4 oz/1 kg lamb fillet, cut into ¾-inch/2-cm pieces

lemon slices, to garnish

Mix the garlic, onion, lemon rind, lemon juice, thyme, coriander, cumin, vinegar, and olive oil together in a large, shallow, nonmetallic dish, whisking well until thoroughly combined.

Thread the pieces of lamb onto 16 wooden skewers and add to the dish, turning well to coat. Cover with plastic wrap and let marinate in the refrigerator for 2–8 hours, turning occasionally.

Preheat the broiler to medium. Drain the skewers, reserving the marinade. Cook under the hot broiler, turning frequently and brushing with the marinade, for 10 minutes, or until tender and cooked to your liking.

Serve immediately, garnished with lemon slices.

Spareribs Coated in Paprika Sauce

serves 6

Spanish olive oil, for oiling

2 lb 12 oz/1.25 kg pork spareribs

⅓ cup dry Spanish sherry

5 tsp hot or sweet smoked Spanish paprika

2 garlic cloves, crushed

1 tbsp dried oregano

⅔ cup water

salt

Preheat the oven to 425°F/220°C. Oil a large roasting pan. If the butcher has not already done so, cut the sheets of spareribs into individual ribs.

If possible, cut each sparerib in half widthwise. Put the spareribs in the prepared pan, in a single layer, and roast in the preheated oven for 20 minutes.

Meanwhile, make the sauce. Put the sherry, paprika, garlic, oregano, water, and salt to taste in a pitcher and mix together well.

Reduce the oven temperature to 350°F/180°C. Pour off the fat from the pan, then pour the sauce over the spareribs and turn the spareribs to coat with the sauce on both sides. Roast for an additional 45 minutes, basting the spareribs with the sauce once halfway through the cooking time, until tender.

Pile the spareribs into a warmed serving dish. Bring the sauce in the roasting pan to a boil on the stove, then reduce the heat and simmer until reduced by half. Pour the sauce over the spareribs and serve hot.

Miniature Pork Brochettes

makes 12

1 lb/450 g lean boneless
pork

3 tbsp olive oil, plus extra
for oiling (optional)

grated rind and juice of
1 large lemon

2 garlic cloves, crushed

2 tbsp chopped fresh
flat-leaf parsley, plus
extra to garnish

1 tbsp ras el hanout
spice blend

salt and pepper

Cut the pork into pieces about ¾-inch/2-cm square and put in a large, shallow, nonmetallic dish that will hold the pieces in a single layer.

To prepare the marinade, put all the remaining ingredients in a bowl and mix well together. Pour the marinade over the pork and toss the meat in it until well coated. Cover the dish and let marinate in the refrigerator for 8 hours or overnight, stirring the pork 2–3 times.

Preheat the broiler to medium–high. Thread 3 marinated pork pieces, leaving a little space between each piece, onto each skewer. Cook the brochettes for 10–15 minutes, or until tender and lightly charred, turning several times and basting with the remaining marinade during cooking. Serve the pork brochettes piping hot, garnished with parsley.

Serrano Ham Croquettes

serves 4

4 tbsp Spanish olive oil

1 small onion, finely chopped

1 garlic clove, crushed

4 tbsp all-purpose flour

scant 1 cup milk

7 oz/200 g Serrano ham or cooked ham, in one piece, finely diced

pinch of hot or sweet smoked Spanish paprika

1 egg

1 cup day-old white breadcrumbs

sunflower oil, for deep-frying

salt

aïoli, for serving

Heat the olive oil in a pan, then add the onion and cook over medium heat, stirring occasionally, for 5 minutes, or until softened but not browned. Add the garlic and cook, stirring, for 30 seconds. Stir in the flour and cook over low heat, stirring constantly, for 1 minute without the mixture coloring. Remove the pan from the heat and gradually stir in the milk to form a smooth sauce. Return to the heat and slowly bring to a boil, stirring constantly, until the sauce boils and thickens.

Remove the pan from the heat, then stir in the ham and paprika and season to taste with salt. Spread the mixture in a shallow dish and let cool, then cover and chill in the refrigerator for at least 2 hours or overnight.

When the mixture has chilled, break the egg onto a plate and beat lightly. Spread the breadcrumbs on a separate plate. Using wet hands, form the ham mixture into 8 even-size pieces and form each piece into a cylindrical shape. Dip the croquettes, one at a time, into the beaten egg, then roll in the breadcrumbs to coat. Put on a plate and chill in the refrigerator for at least 1 hour.

Heat enough sunflower oil for deep-frying in a deep-fat fryer to 350–375°F/180–190°C, or until a cube of bread browns in 30 seconds. Add the croquettes, in batches to avoid overcrowding, and cook for 5 minutes, or until golden brown and crisp. Remove with a slotted spoon or draining basket and drain on paper towels. Keep hot in a warm oven while you cook the remaining croquettes. Serve hot with aïoli.

Empanadillas with Ham & Cheese

serves 16

1 tbsp Spanish olive oil

1 small onion, finely chopped

1 garlic clove, crushed

5½ oz/150 g soft goat cheese

6 oz/175 g thickly sliced cooked ham, finely chopped

scant ½ cup capers, chopped

½ tsp hot or sweet smoked Spanish paprika

1 lb 2 oz/500 g prepared puff pastry, thawed if frozen

all-purpose flour, for dusting

beaten egg, for glazing

salt

Preheat the oven to 400°F/200°C. Dampen several large cookie sheets. Heat the oil in a large skillet, then add the onion and cook over medium heat, stirring occasionally, for 5 minutes, or until softened but not browned. Add the garlic and cook, stirring, for 30 seconds. Put the goat cheese in a bowl, then add the ham, capers, onion mixture, and paprika and mix together well. Season to taste with salt.

Thinly roll out the pastry on a lightly floured counter. Using a plain, 3¼-inch/8-cm round cutter, cut out 32 circles, rerolling the trimmings as necessary. Using a teaspoon, put an equal, small amount of the goat cheese mixture in the center of each pastry circle. Dampen the edges of the pastry with a little water and fold one half over the other to form a crescent and enclose the filling. Pinch the edges together with your fingers to seal, then press with the tines of a fork to seal further. Transfer to the prepared cookie sheets.

With the tip of a sharp knife, make a small slit in the top of each pastry and brush with beaten egg to glaze. Bake in the preheated oven for 15 minutes, or until risen and golden brown. Serve warm.

Mushrooms Stuffed with Spinach & Bacon

serves 4

5 cups fresh baby spinach leaves

4 portobello mushrooms

3 tbsp olive oil

2 oz/55 g rindless bacon, finely diced

2 garlic cloves, crushed

1 cup fresh white or brown breadcrumbs

2 tbsp chopped fresh basil

salt and pepper

Preheat the oven to 400°F/200°C. Rinse the spinach and place in a pan with only the water clinging to the leaves. Cook for 2–3 minutes, until wilted. Drain, squeezing out as much liquid as possible, and chop finely.

Cut the stalks from the mushrooms and chop finely, reserving the whole caps.

Heat 2 tablespoons of the oil in a skillet. Add the mushroom caps, rounded-side down, and cook for 1 minute. Remove from the skillet and arrange, rounded-side down, in a large ovenproof dish.

Add the chopped mushroom stalks, bacon, and garlic to the skillet and cook for 5 minutes. Stir in the spinach, breadcrumbs, basil, and salt and pepper to taste. Mix well and divide the stuffing among the mushroom caps.

Drizzle the remaining oil over the top and bake in the oven for 20 minutes, until crisp and golden.

Chorizo in Red Wine

serves 6

7 oz/200 g chorizo sausage

¾ cup Spanish red wine

2 tbsp brandy (optional)

fresh flat-leaf parsley sprigs, to garnish

crusty bread, to serve

Using a fork, prick the chorizo in 3 or 4 places. Place the chorizo and wine in a large pan. Bring the wine to a boil, then reduce the heat and simmer gently, covered, for 15–20 minutes. Transfer the chorizo and wine to a bowl or dish, cover, and let the sausage marinate in the wine for 8 hours or overnight.

Remove the chorizo from the bowl or dish and reserve the wine. Remove the outer casing from the chorizo and cut the sausage into ¼-inch/5-mm slices. Place the slices in a large, heavy-bottom skillet or flameproof serving dish.

If you are adding the brandy, pour it into a small pan and heat gently. Pour the brandy over the chorizo slices, then stand well back and set aflame. When the flames have died down, shake the pan gently and add the reserved wine to the pan, then cook over high heat until almost all of the wine has evaporated.

Serve the chorizo in red wine piping hot in the dish in which it was cooked, sprinkled with parsley to garnish. Accompany with chunks or slices of bread to mop up the juices and provide wooden toothpicks to spear the pieces of chorizo.

Chickpeas & Chorizo

serves 4–6

9 oz/250 g chorizo sausage in 1 piece, outer casing removed

4 tbsp Spanish olive oil

1 onion, finely chopped

1 large garlic clove, crushed

14 oz/400 g canned chickpeas, drained and rinsed

6 pimientos del piquillo, drained, patted dry, and sliced

1 tbsp sherry vinegar, or to taste

salt and pepper

finely chopped fresh parsley, to garnish

crusty bread, to serve

Cut the chorizo into ½-inch/1-cm dice. Heat the oil in a heavy-bottom skillet over medium heat, then add the onion and garlic. Cook, stirring occasionally, until the onion is softened but not browned. Stir in the chorizo and cook until heated through.

Transfer the mixture to a bowl and stir in the chickpeas and pimientos. Splash with sherry vinegar and season to taste with salt and pepper. Serve hot or at room temperature, generously sprinkled with parsley, with plenty of crusty bread.

Spicy Fried Bread & Chorizo

serves 6–8

7 oz/200 g chorizo sausage, outer casing removed

4 thick slices 2-day-old country bread

Spanish olive oil, for pan-frying

3 garlic cloves, finely chopped

fresh flat-leaf parsley sprigs and paprika, to garnish

Cut the chorizo into ½-inch/1-cm thick slices and cut the bread, with its crusts still on, into ½-inch/1-cm cubes.

Add enough olive oil to a large, heavy-bottom skillet so that it generously covers the bottom. Heat the oil, then add the garlic and cook for 30 seconds–1 minute, or until lightly browned.

Add the bread cubes to the pan and cook, stirring constantly, until golden brown and crisp. Add the chorizo slices and cook for 1–2 minutes, or until hot. Using a slotted spoon, remove the bread cubes and chorizo from the skillet and drain well on paper towels.

Turn the bread and chorizo into a warmed serving bowl, then add the chopped parsley and toss together. Garnish the dish with parsley sprigs and paprika and serve warm. Accompany with wooden toothpicks so that a piece of sausage and a cube of bread can be speared together for eating.

Chorizo & Mushroom Kebabs

serves 8

2 tbsp Spanish olive oil

24 slices chorizo sausage, each about ½ inch/1 cm thick (about 3½ oz/100 g)

24 button mushrooms, wiped

1 green bell pepper, roasted, peeled, and cut into 24 squares

Heat the olive oil in a skillet over medium heat. Add the chorizo and cook for 20 seconds, stirring.

Add the mushrooms and continue cooking for an additional 1–2 minutes, until the mushrooms begin to brown and absorb the fat in the skillet.

Thread a bell pepper square, a piece of chorizo, and a mushroom onto a wooden toothpick. Continue until all the ingredients are used. Serve hot or at room temperature.

Chicken in Lemon & Garlic

serves 6–8

4 large skinless, boneless chicken breasts

5 tbsp extra virgin olive oil

1 onion, finely chopped

6 garlic cloves, finely chopped

grated rind of 1 lemon, finely pared rind of 1 lemon and juice of both lemons

4 tbsp chopped fresh flat-leaf parsley

salt and pepper

lemon wedges and crusty bread, to serve

Using a sharp knife, slice the chicken breasts widthwise into very thin slices. Heat the olive oil in a large, heavy-bottom skillet, add the onion, and cook for 5 minutes, or until softened but not browned. Add the garlic and cook for an additional 30 seconds.

Add the sliced chicken to the skillet and cook gently for 5–10 minutes, stirring from time to time, until all the ingredients are lightly browned and the chicken is tender.

Add the grated lemon rind and the lemon juice and let it bubble. At the same time, deglaze the skillet by scraping and stirring all the sediment on the bottom of the skillet into the juices with a wooden spoon. Remove the skillet from the heat, stir in the parsley, and season to taste with salt and pepper.

Transfer the chicken in lemon and garlic, piping hot, to a warmed serving dish. Sprinkle with the pared lemon rind, and serve with lemon wedges for squeezing over the chicken, accompanied by chunks or slices of crusty bread for mopping up the lemon and garlic juices.

Chicken Morsels Fried in Batter

serves 6–8

1 lb 2 oz/500 g skinless, boneless chicken thighs

3 tbsp olive oil

juice of ½ lemon

2 garlic cloves, crushed

8 tbsp all-purpose flour

vegetable oil for deep-frying

2 eggs, beaten

salt and pepper

fresh flat-leaf parsley sprigs, to garnish

lemon wedges, to serve

Cut the chicken thighs into 1½-inch/4-cm chunks. Mix the olive oil, lemon juice, and garlic in a bowl and season with salt and pepper. Add the chicken pieces and leave to marinate at room temperature for an hour, or overnight in the refrigerator.

Spread the flour on a plate and mix with a pinch of salt and plenty of pepper.

When ready to cook, remove the chicken pieces from the marinade and drain.

Heat the vegetable oil in a deep-fat fryer or large saucepan until a cube of bread browns in 20 seconds. Roll the chicken in the seasoned flour and then in beaten egg. Immediately drop into the hot oil, a few pieces at a time, and deep-fry for about 5 minutes, until golden and crisp, turning occasionally with tongs. Drain on crumpled paper towels.

Place the chicken pieces in a warmed serving dish and garnish with sprigs of parsley. Serve hot with thick wedges of lemon.

Sautéed Chicken with Crispy Garlic Slices

serves 8

8 skin-on chicken thighs, boned if available

hot or sweet smoked Spanish paprika, to taste

4 tbsp Spanish olive oil

10 garlic cloves, sliced

½ cup dry white wine

1 bay leaf

salt

chopped fresh flat-leaf parsley, to garnish

crusty bread, to serve (optional)

If necessary, halve the chicken thighs and remove the bones, then cut the flesh into bite-size pieces, leaving the skin on. Season to taste with paprika.

Heat the oil in a large skillet or an ovenproof casserole, then add the garlic slices and cook over medium heat, stirring frequently, for 1 minute, or until golden brown. Remove with a slotted spoon and drain on paper towels.

Add the chicken thighs to the skillet and cook, turning occasionally, for 10 minutes, or until tender and golden brown on all sides. Add the wine and bay leaf and bring to a boil. Reduce the heat and simmer, stirring occasionally, for 10 minutes, or until most of the liquid has evaporated and the juices run clear when a skewer is inserted into the thickest part of the meat. Season to taste with salt.

Transfer the chicken to a warmed serving dish and sprinkle over the reserved garlic slices. Sprinkle with parsley to garnish, and serve with chunks of crusty bread to mop up the juices, if using.

Chicken Rolls with Olives

serves 6–8

⅔ cup black Spanish olives in oil, drained and 2 tbsp oil reserved

⅔ cup butter, softened

4 tbsp chopped fresh parsley

4 skinless, boneless chicken breasts

Preheat the oven to 400°F/200°C. Pit and finely chop the olives. Mix the olives, butter, and parsley together in a bowl.

Place the chicken breasts between 2 sheets of plastic wrap and beat gently with a meat mallet or the side of a rolling pin.

Remove from plastic wrap and spread the olive-and-herb butter over one side of each flattened chicken breast and roll up. Secure with a wooden toothpick or tie with clean string if necessary.

Place the chicken rolls in an ovenproof dish. Drizzle over the oil from the olive jar and bake in the preheated oven for 45–55 minutes, or until tender and the juices run clear when the chicken is pierced with the point of a sharp knife.

Transfer the chicken rolls to a cutting board and discard the toothpicks or string. Using a sharp knife, cut into slices, then transfer to warmed serving plates and serve.

Chicken Wings with Tomato Dressing

serves 6–8

¾ cup Spanish olive oil

3 garlic cloves, finely chopped

1 tsp ground cumin

2 lb 4 oz/1 kg chicken wings

2 tomatoes, peeled, seeded, and diced

5 tbsp white wine vinegar

1 tbsp shredded fresh basil leaves

Preheat the oven to 350°F/180°C. Mix 1 tablespoon of the oil with the garlic and cumin in a shallow dish. Cut off and discard the tips of the chicken wings and add the wings to the spice mixture, turning to coat. Cover with plastic wrap and let marinate in a cool place for 15 minutes.

Heat 3 tablespoons of the remaining oil in a large, heavy-bottom skillet. Add the chicken wings, in batches, and cook, turning frequently, until golden brown. Transfer to a roasting pan.

Roast the chicken wings for 10–15 minutes, or until tender and the juices run clear when the point of a sharp knife is inserted into the thickest part of the meat.

Meanwhile, mix the remaining olive oil, the tomatoes, vinegar, and basil together in a bowl.

Using tongs, transfer the chicken wings to a nonmetallic dish. Pour the dressing over them, turning to coat. Cover with plastic wrap and let cool, then chill for 4 hours. Remove from the refrigerator 30–60 minutes before serving to return to room temperature.

Chicken Salad with Raisins & Pine Nuts

serves 6–8

¼ cup red wine vinegar

2 tbsp superfine sugar

1 bay leaf

pared rind of 1 lemon

scant 1 cup seedless raisins

4 large skinless, boneless chicken breasts, about 1 lb 5 oz/600 g in total

5 tbsp Spanish olive oil

1 garlic clove, finely chopped

1 cup pine nuts

⅓ cup Spanish extra virgin olive oil

1 small bunch of fresh flat-leaf parsley, finely chopped

salt and pepper

To make the dressing, put the vinegar, sugar, bay leaf, and lemon rind in a pan and bring to a boil, then remove from the heat. Stir in the raisins and let cool.

When the dressing is cool, slice the chicken breasts widthwise into very thin slices. Heat the olive oil in a large skillet, then add the chicken slices and cook over medium heat, stirring occasionally, for 8–10 minutes, or until lightly browned and tender.

Add the garlic and pine nuts and cook, stirring constantly and shaking the skillet, for 1 minute, or until the pine nuts are golden brown. Season to taste with salt and pepper.

Pour the cooled dressing into a large bowl, discarding the bay leaf and lemon rind. Add the extra virgin olive oil and whisk together. Season to taste with salt and pepper. Add the chicken mixture and parsley and toss together. Turn the salad into a serving dish and serve warm or, if serving cold, cover and chill in the refrigerator for 2–3 hours before serving.

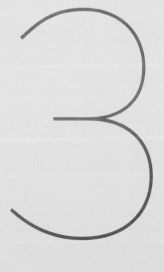

Fish &
Seafood
Dishes

Salt Cod Fritters

serves 16

9 oz/250 g dried salt cod in 1 piece

2 lemon slices

2 fresh parsley sprigs

1 bay leaf

½ tbsp garlic-flavored olive oil

2 cups fresh baby spinach, rinsed

¼ tsp smoked sweet, mild, or hot Spanish paprika, to taste

Spanish olive oil, for frying

coarse sea salt (optional)

aïoli, to serve

for the batter

1 cup all-purpose flour

1 tsp baking powder

¼ tsp salt

1 large egg, lightly beaten

about ⅔ cup milk

To make the batter, sift the flour, baking powder, and salt into a large bowl and make a well. Mix the egg with ½ cup of the milk and pour into the well in the flour, stirring to make a smooth batter with a thick coating consistency. If it seems too thick, gradually stir in the remaining milk, then let stand for at least 1 hour.

Transfer the salt cod to a large skillet set over medium heat. Add the lemon slices, parsley sprigs, bay leaf, and enough water to cover and bring to a boil. Reduce the heat and simmer for 30–45 minutes, or until the fish is tender and flakes easily.

Meanwhile, prepare the spinach. Heat the garlic-flavored olive oil in a small pan over medium heat. Add the spinach with just the water clinging to the leaves and cook for 3–4 minutes, or until wilted. Drain the spinach in a strainer, using the back of a spoon to press out any excess moisture. Finely chop the spinach, then stir it into the batter with the paprika.

Remove the fish from the water and flake the flesh into pieces, removing all the skin and tiny bones. Stir the flesh into the batter.

Heat 2 inches/5 cm of olive oil in a heavy-bottom skillet to 350–375°F/180–190°C, or until a cube of bread browns in 30 seconds. Use a greased tablespoon or measuring spoon to drop spoonfuls of the batter into the oil, then cook for 8–10 minutes, or until golden brown. Work in batches to avoid crowding the skillet. Use a slotted spoon to transfer the fritters to paper towels to drain and sprinkle with sea salt, if using. Serve hot or at room temperature with aïoli for dipping.

Monkfish, Rosemary & Bacon Skewers

serves 6

9 oz/250 g monkfish fillet

12 fresh rosemary stems

3 tbsp olive oil

juice of ½ small lemon

1 garlic clove, crushed

6 rindless thick bacon slices

salt and pepper

lemon wedges, to garnish

aïoli, to serve

Slice the fillet in half lengthwise, then cut each fillet into 12 bite-size chunks to give a total of 24 pieces. Put the monkfish pieces in a large bowl. To prepare the rosemary skewers, strip the leaves off the stems and set them aside, leaving a few leaves at one end.

For the marinade, finely chop the reserved leaves and whisk with the oil, lemon juice, garlic, and salt and pepper to taste in a nonmetallic bowl. Add the fish pieces and toss until coated in the marinade. Cover and let marinate in the refrigerator for 1–2 hours.

Cut each bacon slice in half lengthwise, then in half widthwise, and roll up each piece. Thread 2 fish pieces alternately with 2 bacon rolls onto the prepared rosemary skewers.

Preheat the broiler, griddle, or barbecue. If you are cooking the skewers under a broiler, arrange them on the broiler rack so that the leaves of the rosemary skewers protrude from the broiler and therefore do not catch fire during cooking. Cook the skewers, turning frequently and basting with any remaining marinade, for 10 minutes, or until cooked. Serve hot, garnished with lemon wedges for squeezing over, with some aïoli on the side.

Tuna with Pimiento-Stuffed Olives

serves 6

2 fresh tuna steaks,
weighing about 9 oz/
250 g in total and about
1 inch/2.5 cm thick

5 tbsp olive oil

3 tbsp red wine vinegar

4 sprigs of fresh thyme,
plus extra to garnish

1 bay leaf

2 tbsp all-purpose flour

1 onion, finely chopped

2 garlic cloves, finely
chopped

½ cup pimiento-stuffed
green olives, halved

salt and pepper

Remove the skin from the tuna steaks, then cut the steaks in half along the grain of the fish. Cut each half into ½-inch/1-cm thick slices against the grain.

Put 3 tablespoons of the olive oil and the vinegar in a large, shallow, nonmetallic dish. Strip the leaves from the sprigs of thyme and add these to the dish with the bay leaf and salt and pepper to taste. Add the prepared strips of tuna, cover the dish, and let marinate in the refrigerator for 8 hours or overnight.

The next day, put the flour in a plastic bag. Remove the tuna strips from the marinade, reserving the marinade for later, add them to the bag of flour and toss well until they are lightly coated.

Heat the remaining olive oil in a large, heavy-bottom skillet. Add the onion and garlic and gently cook for 5–10 minutes, or until softened and golden brown. Add the tuna strips to the skillet and cook for 2–5 minutes, turning several times, until the fish becomes opaque. Add the reserved marinade and olives to the skillet and cook for an additional 1–2 minutes, stirring, until the fish is tender and the sauce has thickened.

Serve the tuna and olives piping hot, garnished with thyme sprigs.

Sardines with Romesco Sauce

serves 6

24 fresh sardines, scaled, cleaned, and heads removed

heaping ¾ cup all-purpose flour

4 eggs, lightly beaten

9 oz/250 g fresh white breadcrumbs

6 tbsp chopped fresh parsley

vegetable oil, for deep-frying

for the romesco sauce

1 red bell pepper, halved and seeded

2 tomatoes, halved

4 garlic cloves

½ cup Spanish olive oil

1 slice white bread, diced

4 tbsp blanched almonds

1 fresh red chile, seeded and chopped

2 shallots, chopped

1 tsp paprika

2 tbsp red wine vinegar

2 tsp sugar

First make the sauce. Preheat the oven to 425°F/220°C. Place the bell pepper, tomatoes, and garlic in an ovenproof dish and drizzle over 1 tablespoon of the olive oil, turning to coat. Bake in the preheated oven for 20–25 minutes, then remove from the oven and cool. Peel off their skins and place the flesh in a food processor.

Heat 1 tablespoon of the remaining oil in a skillet. Add the bread and almonds and cook over low heat for a few minutes until browned. Remove and drain on paper towels. Add the chile, shallots, and paprika to the pan and cook for 5 minutes, or until the shallots are softened.

Transfer the almond mixture and shallot mixture to a food processor and add the vinegar, sugar, and just sufficient water to process to a paste. With the motor still running, gradually add the remaining oil through the feeder tube. Transfer to a bowl, cover, and reserve.

Place the sardines, skin-side up, on a cutting board and press along the length of the spines with your thumbs. Turn over and remove and discard the bones. Place the flour and eggs in separate bowls. Mix the breadcrumbs and parsley together in a third bowl. Toss the fish in the flour, the eggs, then in the breadcrumbs.

Heat the vegetable oil in a large pan to 350–375°F/ 180–190°C, or until a cube of bread browns in 30 seconds. Deep-fry the fish for 4–5 minutes, or until golden and tender. Drain and serve with the sauce.

Deep-Fried Whitebait

serves 4

1 lb/450 g fresh whitebait

¾ cup all-purpose flour

1¾ cups cornstarch

½ tsp salt

1 cup cold water

1 egg

a few ice cubes

vegetable oil, for frying

lemon wedges, to serve

for the chili mayonnaise

1 fresh red chile

1 egg yolk

1 tbsp lime juice

2 tbsp chopped fresh cilantro

scant 1 cup light olive oil

salt and pepper

To make the mayonnaise, seed and finely chop the chile and place in a food processor with the egg yolk, lime juice, cilantro, and seasoning. Process until foaming. With the machine still running, gradually add the olive oil, drop by drop, until the mixture begins to thicken. Continue adding the oil in a steady stream until all the oil has been incorporated. Taste and adjust the seasoning and add a little hot water if the mixture is too thick. Set aside.

Rinse the whitebait and pat dry. Set aside on paper towels. Sift together the all-purpose flour, cornstarch, and salt into a large bowl. In a separate bowl, whisk together the water, egg, and ice, then pour onto the flour mix. Whisk briefly until the mixture is runny but still lumpy with dry parts of flour still apparent.

Meanwhile, fill a deep pan about one-third full with vegetable oil and heat to 375°F/190°C, or until a cube of bread browns in 30 seconds.

Dip the whitebait, a few at a time, into the batter and carefully drop into the hot oil. Deep-fry for 1 minutes, until the batter is crisp but not browned. Drain on paper towels and keep warm while you cook the remaining fish. Serve hot with the mayonnaise and lemon wedges.

Mixed Seafood Kebabs with Chili & Lime Glaze

serves 4

16 raw jumbo shrimp, in their shells

12 oz/350 g monkfish or hake fillet

12 oz/350 g salmon fillet, skinned

1-inch/2.5-cm piece fresh ginger

4 tbsp sweet chili sauce

grated rind and juice of 1 lime

sunflower or Spanish olive oil, for oiling (optional)

lime wedges, for serving

Rinse the shrimp under cold running water and pat dry with paper towels. Cut the monkfish and salmon into 1-inch/2.5-cm pieces.

Grate the ginger into a strainer set over a large, nonmetallic bowl to catch the juice. Squeeze the grated ginger to extract all the juice and discard the pulp.

Add the chili sauce and lime rind and juice to the ginger juice and mix together. Add the prepared seafood and stir to coat in the marinade. Cover and let marinate in the refrigerator for 30 minutes.

Meanwhile, if using wooden skewers, soak 8 in cold water for about 30 minutes to help prevent them from burning and the food sticking to them during cooking. If using metal skewers, lightly brush with oil.

Preheat the broiler to high and line the broiler pan with foil. Remove the seafood from the marinade, reserving the remaining marinade, and thread an equal quantity onto each prepared skewer, leaving a little space between each piece. Arrange in the broiler pan. Cook the skewers under the broiler, turning once and brushing with the reserved marinade, for 6–8 minutes, or until cooked through. Serve hot, drizzled with the marinade in the broiler pan and with lime wedges for squeezing over.

Batter-Fried Fish Sticks

serves 6

generous ¾ cup all-purpose flour, plus extra for dusting

pinch of salt

1 egg, beaten

1 tbsp Spanish olive oil

⅔ cup water

1 lb 5 oz/600 g firm-fleshed white fish fillet, such as monkfish or hake

sunflower or Spanish olive oil, for deep-frying

lemon wedges, to serve

To make the batter, put the flour and salt into a large bowl and make a well in the center. Pour the egg and olive oil into the well, then gradually add the water, mixing in the flour from the side and beating constantly, until all the flour is incorporated and a smooth batter forms.

Cut the fish into sticks about ¾ inch/2 cm wide and 2 inches/5 cm long. Dust lightly with flour so that the batter sticks to them when dipped in it.

Heat enough sunflower or olive oil for deep-frying in a deep-fat fryer to 350–375°F/180–190°C, or until a cube of bread browns in 30 seconds. Spear a fish stick onto a toothpick and dip into the batter, then drop the fish and toothpick into the hot oil. Cook the fish sticks, in batches to avoid overcrowding, for 5 minutes, or until golden brown. Remove with a slotted spoon or draining basket and drain on paper towels. Keep hot in a warm oven while cooking the remaining fish sticks. Serve the fish sticks hot, with lemon wedges for squeezing over.

Roman Dip with Anchovy Circles

serves 12

1 egg

scant 1 cup pitted black
Spanish olives

1¾ oz/50 g canned anchovy
fillets in olive oil, drained
and oil set aside

2 garlic cloves, 1 crushed
and 1 peeled, but
kept whole

1 tbsp capers

½ tsp hot or sweet smoked
Spanish paprika

1 tbsp Spanish brandy
or sherry

4 tbsp Spanish extra virgin
olive oil

1 small baguette

pepper

Put the egg in a pan, then cover with cold water and slowly bring to a boil. Reduce the heat and simmer gently for 10 minutes. Immediately drain the egg and rinse under cold running water to cool. Gently tap the egg to crack the shell and let stand until cold.

When the egg is cold, crack the shell all over and remove it. Put the egg in a food processor and add the olives, 2 of the anchovy fillets, the crushed garlic, capers, paprika, and brandy and process to a coarse paste. With the motor running, very slowly add 1 tablespoon of the reserved oil from the anchovies and the extra virgin olive oil in a thin, steady stream. Season the dip to taste with pepper.

Turn the dip into a small serving bowl, then cover and chill in the refrigerator until ready to serve.

To make the anchovy circles, put the remaining anchovy fillets, remaining reserved oil from the anchovies, and garlic clove in a mortar and, using a pestle, pound together to a paste. Turn the paste into a bowl, then cover and chill in the refrigerator until ready to serve.

When ready to serve, preheat the broiler to high. Slice the baguette into 1-inch/2.5-cm circles and toast under the broiler until golden brown on both sides. Spread the anchovy paste very thinly on the toasted bread circles and serve with the dip.

Empanadillas with Tuna & Olives

serves 16

6 oz/175 g canned tuna in olive oil

1 small onion, finely chopped

1 garlic clove, finely chopped

1¾ oz/50 g pimiento-stuffed Spanish olives, finely chopped

heaping 2 tbsp pine nuts

1 lb 2 oz/500 g prepared puff pastry, thawed if frozen

salt and pepper

all-purpose flour, for dusting

beaten egg, for glazing

Drain the tuna, reserving the oil, put in a large bowl, and set aside. Heat 1 tablespoon of the reserved oil from the tuna in a large skillet, then add the onion and cook over medium heat, stirring occasionally, for 5 minutes, or until softened but not browned. Add the garlic and cook, stirring, for 30 seconds, or until softened.

Mash the tuna with a fork, then add the onion mixture, olives, and pine nuts and mix together well. Season to taste with salt and pepper.

Preheat the oven to 400°F/200°C. Dampen several large cookie sheets. Thinly roll out the pastry on a lightly floured counter. Using a plain, 3¼-inch/8-cm round cutter, cut out 32 circles, rerolling the trimmings as necessary. Using a teaspoon, put an equal, small amount of the tuna mixture in the center of each pastry circle.

Dampen the edges of the pastry with a little water and fold one half over the other to form a crescent and enclose the filling. Pinch the edges together with your fingers to seal, then press with the tines of a fork to seal further. Transfer to the prepared cookie sheets.

With the tip of a sharp knife, make a small slit in the top of each pastry and brush with beaten egg to glaze. Bake in the preheated oven for 15 minutes, or until risen and golden brown. Serve warm.

Shrimp & Northern Bean Toasties

serves 4

3 garlic cloves

4 tbsp Spanish olive oil

1 Spanish onion, halved and finely chopped

14 oz/400 g canned great Northern beans, drained and rinsed

4 tomatoes, diced

4 thick slices country bread

10 oz/280 g cooked, shelled shrimp

salt and pepper

watercress, to garnish

Halve 1 of the garlic cloves and reserve. Finely chop the remaining cloves. Heat 2 tablespoons of the olive oil in a large, heavy-bottom skillet. Add the chopped garlic and onion and cook over low heat, stirring occasionally, for 5 minutes, or until softened.

Stir in the beans and tomatoes and season to taste with salt and pepper. Cook gently for an additional 5 minutes.

Meanwhile, toast the bread on both sides, then rub each slice with the cut sides of the reserved garlic and drizzle with the remaining oil.

Stir the shrimp into the bean mixture and heat through gently for 2–3 minutes. Pile the bean-and-shrimp mixture onto the toasts and serve immediately, garnished with watercress.

Pan-Fried Shrimp

serves 4

4 garlic cloves

20–24 large shrimp, peeled

8 tbsp butter

4 tbsp olive oil

6 tbsp brandy

salt and pepper

2 tbsp chopped fresh parsley, to garnish

lemon wedges, to serve

Using a sharp knife, peel and slice the garlic.

Wash the shrimp and pat dry using paper towels.

Melt the butter with the oil in a large skillet, add the garlic and shrimp, and fry over high heat, stirring, for 3–4 minutes, until the shrimp are pink.

Sprinkle with brandy and season with salt and pepper to taste. Sprinkle with parsley and serve immediately with lemon wedges, for squeezing over.

Calamares

serves 6

1 lb/450 g prepared squid

all-purpose flour,
for coating

corn oil, for deep-frying

salt

lemon wedges and sprigs
of fresh flat-leaf parsley,
to garnish

aïoli, to serve

Slice the squid into ½-inch/1-cm rings and halve the tentacles if large. Rinse and dry well on paper towels so that they do not spit during cooking. Dust the squid rings with flour so that they are lightly coated.

Heat the corn oil in a deep-fryer to 350–375°F/180–190°C, or until a cube of bread browns in 30 seconds. Carefully add the squid rings, in batches so that the temperature of the oil does not drop, and deep-fry for 2–3 minutes, or until golden brown and crisp all over, turning several times. Do not overcook or the squid will become tough and rubbery rather than moist and tender.

Using a slotted spoon, remove the deep-fried squid from the deep-fryer and drain well on paper towels. Transfer to a warm oven while you deep-fry the remaining squid rings.

Sprinkle the deep-fried squid with salt and serve piping hot, garnished with lemon wedges for squeezing over and parsley sprigs. Accompany with a bowl of aïoli in which to dip the calamares.

Seared Squid & Golden Potatoes

serves 8

2 lb 4 oz/1 kg new potatoes

4–6 tbsp Spanish olive oil

1 large onion, thinly sliced

2 garlic cloves, finely chopped

2 lb 4 oz/1 kg cleaned squid bodies, thinly sliced

6 tbsp dry white wine

1 small bunch of fresh flat-leaf parsley, finely chopped

salt and pepper

lemon wedges, to serve

Put the potatoes in a pan of water and bring to a boil. Reduce the heat and simmer for 20 minutes, or until tender. Drain well.

Heat 4 tablespoons of oil in a large ovenproof casserole, then add the potatoes and cook over medium heat, stirring occasionally, for 10 minutes, or until beginning to turn brown. Add the onion and cook, stirring occasionally, for 10 minutes, or until golden brown. Add the garlic and cook, stirring, for 30 seconds, until softened. Push all the ingredients to the side of the casserole.

If necessary, add the remaining oil to the casserole. Add the squid slices and cook over high heat, stirring occasionally, for 2 minutes, or until golden brown. Add the wine and cook for an additional 1–2 minutes. Add most of the parsley, reserving a little to garnish, and mix the potatoes, onions, and garlic with the squid. Season to taste with salt and pepper.

Serve hot in the casserole, with the reserved parsley and the lemon wedges.

Scallop Tartlets with Pea & Mint Puree

makes 12

4 oz/115 g prepared puff pastry, rolled to a depth of ⅛ inch/3 mm

4 large fresh scallops, cleaned and roes removed

extra virgin olive oil, for coating

salt and pepper

for the pea & mint puree

⅓ cup cooked peas

small garlic clove, grated

1 tbsp extra virgin olive oil

1 tbsp chopped mint

1 tbsp sour cream

1 tsp lemon juice

salt and pepper

Preheat the oven to 350°F/180°C. Using a 1½-inch/4-cm round cookie cutter, cut out 12 pastry circles. Reroll and use the leftovers if there is not enough pastry to make 12 circles.

Place the circles on a cookie sheet lined with wax paper. Place another layer of wax paper on top, and then place a slightly smaller cookie sheet on top of this. (This will prevent the pastry from rising in the oven.)

Set aside the pastry circles to rest in a cool place for 20 minutes, then cook in the oven for 15–20 minutes, or until golden. Remove from the oven and let cool.

To make the pea and mint puree, blend the peas in a food processor and add the garlic, olive oil, mint, sour cream, lemon juice, and salt and pepper to taste. Process until combined. Scrape the mixture into a small container and place in the refrigerator.

Heat a nonstick skillet until just smoking. Toss the scallops in a little olive oil and season with salt and pepper. Add the scallops to the skillet and cook for 30 seconds each side. Remove the scallops from the pan and set aside.

To assemble, place a small amount of pea and mint puree on each tartlet. Cut each scallop into 3 slices and arrange on top.

Scallops with Serrano Ham

serves 4

2 tbsp lemon juice

3 tbsp Spanish olive oil

2 garlic cloves, finely chopped

1 tbsp chopped fresh parsley

12 shelled scallops, preferably with corals

8 wafer-thin slices Serrano ham

pepper

Mix the lemon juice, olive oil, garlic, and parsley together in a nonmetallic dish. Separate the corals, if using, from the scallops and add both to the dish, turning to coat. Cover with plastic wrap and let marinate at room temperature for 20 minutes.

Preheat the broiler to medium. Drain the scallops, reserving the marinade. Thread a scallop and a coral, if using, onto a metal skewer. Scrunch up a slice of ham and thread onto the skewer, followed by another scallop and a coral. Repeat to fill 4 skewers, each with 3 scallops and 2 slices of ham.

Cook under the hot broiler, basting with the marinade and turning frequently, for 5 minutes, or until the scallops are tender and the ham is crisp.

Transfer to warmed serving plates and sprinkle them with pepper. Spoon over the cooking juices from the broiler pan and serve.

Sweet Bell Peppers Stuffed with Crab Salad

serves 8

16 pimientos del piquillo, drained, or freshly roasted sweet peppers, tops cut off

chopped fresh parsley, to garnish

for the crab salad

8½ oz/240 g canned crabmeat, drained and squeezed dry

1 red bell pepper, roasted, peeled, and chopped

about 2 tbsp fresh lemon juice

scant 1 cup cream cheese

salt and pepper

First make the crab salad. Pick over the crabmeat and remove any pieces of shell. Put half the crabmeat in a food processor with the prepared red bell pepper, 1½ tablespoons of the lemon juice, and salt and pepper to taste. Process until well blended, then transfer to a bowl. Flake and stir in the remaining crabmeat along with the cream cheese.

Pat the pimientos del piquillo dry and scoop out any seeds that remain in the tips. Use a small spoon to divide the crab salad equally among the pimientos, stuffing them generously. Arrange on a large serving dish or individual plates, then cover and let chill until ready to serve. Just before serving, sprinkle the stuffed pimientos with the chopped parsley.

Mussels with Herb & Garlic Butter

serves 8

1 lb 12 oz/800 g fresh mussels, in their shells

splash of dry white wine

1 bay leaf

6 tbsp butter

generous ¼ cup fresh white or brown breadcrumbs

4 tbsp chopped fresh flat-leaf parsley, plus extra sprigs to garnish

2 tbsp snipped fresh chives

2 garlic cloves, finely chopped

salt and pepper

lemon wedges, to serve

Clean the mussels by scrubbing or scraping the shells and pulling out any beards that are attached to them. Discard any with broken shells and any that refuse to close when tapped. Put the mussels in a strainer and rinse well under cold running water. Preheat the oven to 450°F/230°C.

Put the mussels in a large pan and add a splash of wine and the bay leaf. Cook, covered, over high heat for 5 minutes, shaking the pan occasionally, or until the mussels are opened. Drain the mussels and discard any that remain closed.

Shell the mussels, reserving one half of each shell. Arrange the mussels, in their half shells, in a large, shallow, ovenproof serving dish.

Melt the butter and pour into a small bowl. Add the breadcrumbs, parsley, chives, garlic, and salt and pepper to taste and mix well together. Let stand until the butter has set slightly. Using your fingers or 2 teaspoons, take a large pinch of the herb-and-butter mixture and use to fill each mussel shell, pressing it down well. You can chill the filled mussels in the refrigerator at this point until ready to serve.

To serve, bake the mussels in the oven for 10 minutes, or until hot. Serve immediately, garnished with parsley sprigs, and accompanied by lemon wedges, for squeezing over them.

Clams in Tomato & Garlic Sauce

serves 6–8

2 hard-cooked eggs, cooled, shelled, and halved lengthwise

3 tbsp Spanish olive oil

1 Spanish onion, chopped

2 garlic cloves, finely chopped

1 lb 9 oz/700 g tomatoes, peeled and diced

3/4 cup fresh white breadcrumbs

2 lb 4 oz/1 kg fresh clams

1 3/4 cups dry white wine

2 tbsp chopped fresh parsley

salt and pepper

lemon wedges, to garnish

Scoop out the egg yolks using a teaspoon and rub through a fine strainer into a bowl. Chop the whites and reserve separately.

Heat the olive oil in a large, heavy-bottom skillet. Add the onion and cook over low heat, stirring occasionally, for 5 minutes, or until softened. Add the garlic and cook for an additional 3 minutes, then add the tomatoes, breadcrumbs, and egg yolks and season to taste with salt and pepper. Cook, stirring occasionally and mashing the mixture with a wooden spoon, for an additional 10–15 minutes, or until thick and pulpy.

Meanwhile, scrub the clams under cold running water. Discard any with broken shells or any that do not close immediately when sharply tapped with the back of a knife.

Place the clams in a large, heavy-bottom pan. Add the wine and bring to a boil. Cover and cook over high heat, shaking the pan occasionally, for 3–5 minutes, or until the clams have opened. Discard any that remain closed.

Using a slotted spoon, transfer the clams to warmed serving bowls. Strain the cooking liquid into the tomato sauce, then stir well and spoon over the clams. Sprinkle with the chopped egg whites and parsley and serve immediately, garnished with lemon wedges.

4

Egg & Cheese Dishes

Spanish Tortilla

serves 8

½ cup Spanish olive oil

1 lb 5 oz/600 g potatoes,
peeled and thinly sliced

1 large onion, thinly sliced

6 large eggs

salt and pepper

fresh flat-leaf parsley,
to garnish

Heat a nonstick 10-inch/25-cm skillet over high heat.
Add the olive oil and heat. Reduce the heat, then add the
potatoes and onion and cook for 15–20 minutes, or until
the potatoes are tender.

Beat the eggs in a large bowl and season generously with
salt and pepper. Drain the potatoes and onion through
a strainer over a heatproof bowl to reserve the oil. Very
gently stir the vegetables into the eggs, then let stand
for 10 minutes.

Use a wooden spoon or spatula to remove any crusty
sediment stuck to the bottom of the skillet. Reheat the
skillet over medium heat with 4 tablespoons of the reserved
oil. Add the egg mixture and smooth the surface, pressing
the potatoes and onions into an even layer.

Cook for 5 minutes, shaking the skillet occasionally, until
the bottom is set. Use a spatula to loosen the side of the
tortilla. Place a large plate over the top and carefully
invert the skillet and plate together so the tortilla drops
onto the plate.

Add 1 tablespoon of the remaining reserved oil to the skillet
and swirl around. Carefully slide the tortilla back into the
skillet, cooked-side up. Run the spatula around the tortilla
to tuck in the edge.

Continue cooking for 3 minutes, or until the eggs are set
and the bottom is golden brown. Remove the skillet from
the heat and slide the tortilla onto a plate. Let stand for
at least 5 minutes before cutting. Garnish with parsley
and serve.

Oven-Baked Tortilla

serves 16

4 tbsp Spanish olive oil,
plus extra for oiling

1 large garlic clove, crushed

4 scallions, white and
green parts finely
chopped

1 green bell pepper, seeded
and finely diced

1 red bell pepper, seeded
and finely diced

6 oz/175 g potato, boiled,
peeled, and diced

5 large eggs

scant ½ cup sour cream

6 oz/175 g Spanish Rocal,
cheddar, or Parmesan
cheese, grated

3 tbsp snipped fresh chives

salt and pepper

slices of bread, to serve

Preheat the oven to 375°F/190°C. Line a 7 x 10-inch/
18 x 25-cm baking sheet with foil and brush with a little
olive oil. Reserve.

Place the olive oil, garlic, scallions, and bell peppers in a
skillet and cook over medium heat, stirring, for 10 minutes,
or until the onions are softened but not browned. Let cool,
then stir in the potato.

Beat the eggs, sour cream, cheese, and chives together in
a large bowl. Stir the cooled vegetables into the bowl and
season to taste with salt and pepper.

Pour the mixture into the baking sheet and smooth over
the top. Bake in the preheated oven for 30–40 minutes,
or until golden brown, puffed, and set in the center. Remove
from the oven and let cool and set. Run a spatula around
the edge, then invert onto a cutting board, browned-side
up, and peel off the foil. If the surface looks a little runny,
place it under a medium broiler to dry out.

Let cool completely. Trim the edges if necessary, then cut
into 48 squares. Serve on a platter with wooden toothpicks,
or secure each square to a slice of bread.

Tomato & Potato Tortilla

serves 6

2 lb 4 oz/1 kg potatoes, peeled and cut into small cubes

2 tbsp olive oil

1 bunch of scallions, chopped

4 oz/115 g cherry tomatoes, halved

6 eggs

3 tbsp water

2 tbsp chopped fresh parsley

salt and pepper

Cook the potatoes in a saucepan of lightly salted boiling water for 8–10 minutes, or until tender. Drain and set aside until required.

Preheat the broiler to medium. Heat the oil in a large skillet with a heatproof handle. Add the scallions and cook until just softened. Add the potatoes and cook for 3–4 minutes, until coated with oil and hot. Smooth the top and sprinkle the tomatoes throughout.

Mix the eggs, water, parsley, and seasoning in a bowl, then pour into the skillet. Cook over very gentle heat for 10–15 minutes, until the tortilla looks fairly set.

Place the skillet under the hot broiler and cook until the top is brown and set. Cool for 10–15 minutes before sliding out of the skillet onto a cutting board. Cut into wedges and serve at once.

Flamenco Eggs

serves 4

4 tbsp Spanish olive oil

1 onion, thinly sliced

2 garlic cloves, finely
chopped

2 small red bell peppers,
seeded and chopped

4 tomatoes, peeled, seeded,
and chopped

1 tbsp chopped fresh
parsley

salt and cayenne pepper

7 oz/200 g canned corn
kernels, drained

4 eggs

Preheat the oven to 350°F/180°C. Heat the olive oil in a large, heavy-bottom skillet. Add the onion and garlic and cook over low heat, stirring occasionally, for 5 minutes, or until softened. Add the red bell peppers and cook, stirring occasionally, for an additional 10 minutes. Stir in the tomatoes and parsley, season to taste with salt and cayenne pepper, and cook for an additional 5 minutes. Stir in the corn kernels and remove the skillet from the heat.

Divide the mixture among 4 individual ovenproof dishes. Make a hollow in the surface of each using the back of a spoon. Break an egg into each depression.

Bake in the preheated oven for 15–25 minutes, or until the eggs have set. Serve hot.

Deviled Eggs

makes 16

8 large eggs

2 whole pimientos (sweet red peppers) from a jar or can

8 green olives

5 tbsp mayonnaise

8 drops Tabasco sauce

large pinch cayenne pepper

salt and pepper

paprika, for dusting

sprigs of fresh dill, to garnish

To cook the eggs, put them in a pan, cover with cold water, and slowly bring to a boil. Immediately reduce the heat to very low, cover, and let simmer gently for 10 minutes. As soon as the eggs are cooked, drain, and put under cold running water. By doing this quickly, you will prevent a black ring from forming around the egg yolk. Gently tap the eggs to crack the eggshells and let them stand until cold. When cold, crack the shells all over and remove them.

Using a stainless steel knife, halve the eggs lengthwise, then carefully remove the yolks. Put the yolks in a nylon strainer, set over a bowl, and rub through, then mash them with a wooden spoon or fork. If necessary, rinse the egg whites under cold water and dry very carefully.

Put the pimientos on paper towels to dry well, then chop them finely, reserving a few strips. Finely chop the olives, but reserve 16 larger pieces of each to garnish. If you are going to pipe the filling into the eggs, you need to chop both these ingredients very finely so that they will go through a 1/2-inch/1-cm tip. Add the finely chopped pimientos and olives to the mashed egg yolks. Add the mayonnaise, mix well together, then add the Tabasco sauce, cayenne pepper, and salt and pepper to taste.

Using a teaspoon, spoon the prepared filling into each egg half. Arrange the eggs on a serving plate and add a small strip of the reserved pimientos and a piece of olive to the top of each stuffed egg. Garnish with dill sprigs and serve.

Egg & Tapenade Toasts

makes 8

1 small baguette

4 tomatoes, thinly sliced

4 hard-cooked eggs

4 bottled or canned anchovies in olive oil, drained and halved lengthwise

8 marinated pitted black olives

for the tapenade

½ cup pitted black olives

6 bottled or canned anchovies in olive oil, drained

2 tbsp capers, rinsed

2 garlic cloves, coarsely chopped

1 tsp Dijon mustard

2 tbsp lemon juice

1 tsp fresh thyme leaves

4–5 tbsp olive oil

pepper

To make the tapenade, place the olives, anchovies, capers, garlic, mustard, lemon juice, thyme, and pepper to taste in a food processor and process for 20–25 seconds, or until smooth. Scrape down the sides of the mixing bowl. With the motor running, gradually add the oil through the feeder tube to make a smooth paste. Spoon the paste into a bowl, cover with plastic wrap, and set aside until required.

Preheat the broiler to medium. Cut the baguette into 8 slices, discarding the crusty ends. Toast on both sides under the hot broiler until light golden brown. Let cool.

To assemble the toasts, spread a little of the tapenade on 1 side of each slice of toast. Top with the tomato slices. Shell the hard-cooked eggs, then slice and arrange over the tomatoes. Dot each egg slice with a little of the remaining tapenade and top with anchovies. Halve the marinated olives and arrange 2 halves on each toast. Serve immediately.

Chorizo & Quail Egg Toasts

serves 6

12 slices of baguette, sliced
on the diagonal, about
¼ inch/5 mm thick

about 1½ oz/40 g cured,
ready-to-eat chorizo, cut
into thin slices

olive oil

12 quail eggs

mild paprika, for dusting

salt and pepper

Preheat the broiler to high. Arrange the slices of bread on a baking sheet and broil until golden brown on both sides.

Cut or fold the chorizo slices to fit on the toasts; set aside. Heat a thin layer of oil in a large skillet over medium heat until a cube of day-old bread sizzles—this takes about 40 seconds. Break the eggs into the skillet and cook, spooning the fat over the yolks, until the whites are set and the yolks are cooked to your liking.

Remove the cooked eggs from the skillet and drain on paper towels. Immediately transfer to the chorizo-topped toasts and dust with paprika. Sprinkle with salt and pepper to taste, and serve at once.

Empanadillas with Cheese & Olives

serves 6

3 oz/85 g firm or soft cheese

½ cup pitted green Spanish olives

⅓ cup sun-dried tomatoes in oil, drained

1¾ oz/50 g canned anchovy fillets, drained

2 oz/55 g sun-dried tomato paste

1 lb 2 oz/500 g prepared puff pastry, thawed if frozen

all-purpose flour, for dusting

beaten egg, for glazing

pepper

Preheat the oven to 400°F/200°C. Cut the cheese into small dice measuring about ¼ inch/5 mm. Chop the olives, sun-dried tomatoes, and anchovies into pieces about the same size as the cheese. Place all the chopped ingredients in a bowl, then season to taste with pepper and gently mix together. Stir in the sun-dried tomato paste.

Thinly roll out the puff pastry on a lightly floured counter. Using a plain, round 3¼-inch/8-cm cutter, cut into 16 circles. Gently pile the trimmings together and roll out again, then cut out an additional 8 circles. Using a teaspoon, place a little of the prepared filling equally in the center of each of the pastry circles.

Dampen the edges of the pastry with a little water, then bring up the sides to completely cover the filling and pinch the edges together with your fingers to seal them. With the point of a sharp knife, make a small slit in the top of each pastry. You can store the pastries in the refrigerator at this stage until you are ready to bake them.

Place the pastries onto dampened baking sheets and brush each with a little beaten egg to glaze. Bake in the preheated oven for 10–15 minutes, or until golden brown, crisp, and well risen. Serve the empanadillas piping hot, warm, or cold.

Sun-Dried Tomato & Goat Cheese Tarts

serves 6

2½ oz/70 g sun-dried tomatoes in oil, drained and 2 tbsp oil reserved

1 zucchini, thinly sliced

1 garlic clove, crushed

9 oz/250 g puff pastry, thawed if frozen

all-purpose flour, for dusting

5½ oz/150 g soft goat cheese

salt and pepper

Preheat the oven to 425°F/220°C. Dampen a large cookie sheet. Finely chop the sun-dried tomatoes and reserve. Heat 1 tablespoon of the reserved oil from the tomatoes in a large skillet, then add the zucchini slices and cook over medium heat, stirring occasionally, for 8–10 minutes, or until golden brown on both sides. Add the garlic and cook, stirring, for 30 seconds. Remove from the heat and let cool while you prepare the pastry bases.

Thinly roll out the pastry on a lightly floured counter. Using a plain, 3½-inch/9-cm cutter, cut out 1–2 circles, rerolling the trimmings as necessary. Transfer the circles to the prepared cookie sheet and prick 3–4 times with the tines of a fork. Divide the zucchini mixture equally among the pastry circles, add the tomatoes, leaving a ½-inch/1-cm border around the edge, and top each tart with a spoonful of goat cheese. Drizzle over 1 tablespoon of the remaining oil from the tomatoes and season to taste with salt and pepper.

Bake the tarts in the preheated oven for 10–15 minutes, or until golden brown and well risen. Serve warm.

Deep-Fried Manchego Cheese

serves 6–8

7 oz/200 g Manchego cheese

3 tbsp all-purpose flour

1 egg

1 tsp water

1½ cups fresh white or brown breadcrumbs

corn oil, for deep-frying

salt and pepper

Slice the cheese into triangular shapes about ¾ inch/2 cm thick or alternatively into cubes measuring about the same size. Put the flour in a plastic bag and season with salt and pepper to taste. Break the egg into a shallow dish and beat together with the water. Spread the breadcrumbs onto a plate.

Toss the cheese pieces in the flour so that they are evenly coated, then dip the cheese in the egg mixture. Finally, dip the cheese in the breadcrumbs so that the pieces are coated on all sides. Transfer to a large plate and store in the refrigerator until you are ready to serve them.

Just before serving, heat about 1 inch/2.5 cm of the corn oil in a large, heavy-bottom skillet or heat the oil in a deep-fryer to 350–375°F/180–190°C, or until a cube of bread browns in 30 seconds. Add the cheese pieces, in batches of about 4 or 5 pieces so that the temperature of the oil does not drop, and deep-fry for 1–2 minutes, turning once, until the cheese is just starting to melt and they are golden brown on all sides. Make sure that the oil is hot enough, otherwise the coating on the cheese will take too long to become crisp and the cheese inside may ooze out.

Using a slotted spoon, remove the deep-fried cheese from the skillet or deep-fryer and drain well on paper towels. Serve the deep-fried cheese pieces hot, accompanied by wooden toothpicks, to spear them.

Bell Peppers with Fiery Cheese

serves 6

1 red bell pepper, halved and seeded

1 orange bell pepper, halved and seeded

1 yellow bell pepper, halved and seeded

4 oz/115 g Afuega'l Pitu cheese or other hot spicy cheese, diced

1 tbsp honey

1 tbsp sherry vinegar

salt and pepper

Preheat the broiler to high. Place the bell peppers, skin-side up, in a single layer on a baking sheet. Cook under the hot broiler for 8–10 minutes, or until the skins have blistered and blackened. Using tongs, transfer to a plastic bag. Tie the top and let cool.

When the bell peppers are cool enough to handle, peel off the skin with your fingers or a knife and discard it. Place on a serving dish and sprinkle over the cheese.

Whisk the honey and vinegar together in a bowl and season to taste with salt and pepper. Pour the dressing over the bell peppers, then cover and let chill until ready to serve.

Figs with Bleu Cheese

serves 6

12 ripe figs

12 oz/350 g Spanish bleu cheese, such as Picós, crumbled

Spanish extra virgin olive oil, for drizzling

for the caramelized almonds

½ cup superfine sugar

¾ cup whole almonds

butter, for greasing

First make the caramelized almonds. Place the sugar in a pan over medium heat and stir until the sugar melts and turns golden brown and bubbles. Do not stir once the mixture begins to bubble. Remove the pan from the heat, then add the almonds one at a time and quickly turn with a fork until coated. If the caramel hardens, return the pan to the heat. Transfer each almond to a lightly greased baking sheet once it is coated. Let stand until cool and firm.

To serve, slice the figs in half and arrange 4 halves on individual serving plates. Coarsely chop the almonds by hand. Place a mound of bleu cheese on each plate and sprinkle with the chopped almonds. Drizzle the figs very lightly with the olive oil.

Bleu Cheese & Bean Salad

serves 4

scant 1 cup small dried
great Northern beans,
soaked for 4 hours
or overnight

1 bay leaf

4 tbsp Spanish olive oil

2 tbsp sherry vinegar

2 tsp honey

1 tsp Dijon mustard

2 tbsp toasted slivered
almonds

7 oz/200 g Cabrales or other
bleu cheese, crumbled

salt and pepper

Drain the beans and place in a large, heavy-bottom pan. Pour in enough water to cover, then add the bay leaf and bring to a boil. Boil for 1–1½ hours, or until tender. Drain, then turn into a bowl and let cool slightly. Remove and discard the bay leaf.

Meanwhile, make the dressing. Whisk the olive oil, vinegar, honey, and mustard together in a bowl and season to taste with salt and pepper. Pour the dressing over the beans and toss lightly. Add the almonds and toss lightly again. Let cool to room temperature.

Spoon the beans into individual serving bowls and scatter over the cheese before serving.